# LIZA'S STORY

## Neglect and the Police

by Deborah Anderson
and Martha Finne

Illustrated by Jeanette Swofford

Dillon Press, Inc.   Minneapolis, Minnesota  55415

*To our children: Casey, Erika, Selene, and Elizabeth*

*Illustrations courtesy of Hennepin County Medical Society Auxiliary, Inc.*

Library of Congress Cataloging in Publication Data

Anderson, Deborah.
  Liza's story.

  Summary: Presents a case of child neglect in which the police became involved, demonstrating the positive effect of reporting abuse to caring people.
  1. Child abuse—Investigation—Juvenile literature.  2. Interviewing child abuse—Juvenile literature.  3. Child abuse—Prevention—Juvenile literature.  [1. Child abuse]  I. Finne, Martha.  II. Title.
  HV8079.C46A54  1986        362.7'044        85-25379
  ISBN 0-87518-323-9

Dillon Press, Inc., 242 Portland Avenue South
Minneapolis, Minnesota 55415

Printed in the United States of America
1  2  3  4  5  6  7  8  9  10  95  94  93  92  91  90  89  88  87  86

# Contents

# Liza's Story

"Someone should do something about that girl," Liza's neighbors would say to one another. "Who's watching her? Doesn't anyone make her put on clean clothes or go home for lunch and supper? She sure looks neglected. And her behavior is terrible for a nine year old. What a troublemaker!"

Liza Sutton really seemed like a troublemaker. Sometimes she was helpful and lovable. More often, she was thinking up ways to make trouble. The other kids in the neighborhood often went right along with Liza.

It was Liza's idea to have all the kids knock on doors at night and then run away. She told everyone to roll huge snowballs into the road to block the way. Liza was the one who first threw crab apples at passing cars from the hill near the road.

When the other children did these things, their parents disciplined them. But no one disciplined Liza. Her father worked during the day, and Liza was alone until he came home. Even when he was home, Mr. Sutton didn't spend much time with Liza. The neighbors came over to tell him about Liza's behavior, but he just shrugged. He didn't seem to care that she was doing bad things.

At night, Mr. Sutton would often come home from work and sit in front of the TV. Many times Liza would ask about supper, but Mr. Sutton would say, "I'm not hungry—you go ahead and eat." If Liza wasn't home at suppertime, he didn't call or look for her—he just let her eat when she wanted and go where she wanted. He hardly ever talked to her, even when she skipped school or did something that the neighbors complained about.

The neighbors didn't talk with Liza about her behavior, either. Liza's mother had died two years ago, and everyone felt sorry for Liza. Because of this, they didn't yell at Liza or talk with her about misbehaving. No one knew what to say to her.

Liza felt happiest when she was misbehaving. She liked it when she could make an adult get angry. She liked it when the other kids did what she said. Since no one told her to stop making trouble, her behavior got worse and worse.

Liza's two best friends were Jack and Ben. They were always together. Often they were just having fun—building forts, going swimming, playing baseball,

and pretending to be cops and robbers. But many times they were making trouble together. The trouble soon became more serious.

These three used a knife to cut Mr. Kerner's garden hose after he yelled at them for riding bikes over his flowers. They started a fire while they were playing that burned a part of the woods in their neighborhood. They also stole things like candy bars from the stores in the neighborhood.

One summer night, Liza, Ben and Jack decided to camp out. Then, they planned to sneak around late at night. Nobody would be up, and they would have the whole neighborhood to themselves. They could go through everyone's yard, take a boat for a ride, or do whatever else they wanted. It would be lots of fun, and no one would know.

Of course, they knew this was wrong. They knew their parents would not like this at all. They decided to do it anyway. Erica, a new girl in the neighborhood, wanted to come, too.

Liza went to Erica's house at one o'clock in the morning to wake her up. Erica had left a flashlight outside her window to flash in her face. That didn't work. Erica didn't wake up. So Liza broke into Erica's house and went to Erica's room. She shook Erica and told her to wake up.

Erica's parents heard the noise Liza and Erica made. Liza hid when she heard Erica's parents coming. But Erica's mother found Liza. Both of Erica's parents were very angry. They shouted at the girls. In the end, though, they told Liza to go right home. They didn't try to call Liza's father.

But Liza didn't go home. Instead, she met up with Jack and Ben down the road. She told them what had happened at Erica's house. Even though they were scared now, they decided to sneak around anyway.

Liza felt angry about getting caught at Erica's house. She thought up some really bad things to do that night. The three of them used an old lipstick they found to write on neighbors' cars. They dug up people's gardens and threw tomatoes. Mr. Simak woke up when he heard the noise that Liza, Jack, and Ben made while walking through his yard. The three children also did a very dangerous thing—they played in someone's boat without permission as it floated on the dark lake.

Finally, Ben and Jack went back to their tent. Liza crept into the porch at her house. They thought they were safe again. They thought no one would know.

The next day, though, they were in very big trouble. All the neighbors were

trying to wash lipstick off their cars, but they couldn't. And Mr. Simak had seen them and had told the police! Ben called Liza up to tell her. He said, "We all have to go to the police station. My mom said we'll pick you up. Jack's mom is bringing him. We'll be there in ten minutes. Mom said to be ready when we come."

When Ben and his mother came, Ben's mother honked the horn. Liza came out to the car. Ben was in the back seat, and Liza got in next to him. Everybody was very quiet. Ben and Liza just looked at each other with scared faces.

Liza had never been to the police station. It was near a store where Liza and the boys had stolen candy. She had always wondered what the station looked like inside. Now she was too scared to wonder.

Ben's mother stopped the car in front of the police station. She said, "Let's go in now."

Ben and Liza walked slowly into the police station. Jack and his mother were already there, sitting in chairs just inside the door. Liza and Ben didn't say anything to Jack. They just looked at him, and he looked back at them.

Liza was so afraid that her face was pale, and she had red spots on her neck. Her stomach felt sick. With all her heart she wished she were at home.

Jack's mother went up to the big glass window and said to a lady behind the window, "We're all here now. Would you please tell Officer Myers?"

Liza could see Officer Myers behind the big glass window. He said something to the lady. There was a click and a buzz, and the door swung open. Officer Myers walked up to them and said, "You can all come in to my office. Right this way."

He led them to a small office. Liza looked around. There was a desk with papers and a telephone on it. The police officer put some chairs in front of the desk for them, and then sat down behind the desk in his chair.

Looking right at Ben, Jack, and Liza, Officer Myers said, "Would you be willing to tell me what the three of you were doing last night?"

Jack said slowly, "We did some things we weren't supposed to."

Officer Myers said, "Start from the

beginning and tell me everything that
happened."

Jack, Liza, and Ben each told a part of
the story. Each of them talked quietly
and looked at the floor. Sometimes
Officer Myers had to ask them to speak
more loudly so that he could hear them.

It was hard for the three children to tell about what they did. Finally, they were done. After they finished talking, Officer Myers leaned forward and looked very serious. He said, "When I was your age and kids did bad things, they were hit with a big belt." All three kids looked scared. Liza was afraid that he might hit her with a belt.

"But today," said Officer Myers, "the police cannot hit children. We have to try to understand why children are misbehaving."

Officer Myers then started talking, mostly to Ben's and Jack's mothers. Their mothers told Officer Myers that Jack and Ben would have to tell the neighbors that they were sorry and would have to fix the damage they caused.

Then Officer Myers said, "What about Liza?" Officer Myers knew Liza's mother had died. For a minute everyone was quiet. It hurt Liza to have everyone notice that she did not have a parent there. No one said anything about her mother, but she knew that's who they were thinking about.

Ben's mother told Officer Myers that Liza was "neglected." Jack's mother said, "Liza's father works during the day, so she stays alone."

"Well," said Officer Myers, "I'll go see Mr. Sutton this evening." He turned to Liza and said, "Liza, please tell your father that I'll be calling him. Say that

I'll call soon after he comes home, okay?" Liza felt ashamed and thought she was going to cry. She didn't want to cry in front of everyone, so she shook her head yes, she would tell him.

Until late that afternoon, Liza waited for her dad. He finally came home from work. She told him she had gotten into some trouble. "Officer Myers is going to call you," she said to him.

Liza's dad asked, "What kind of trouble?" Liza could only say, "It was bad trouble," and she couldn't talk anymore. She only looked at the floor and felt sad and ashamed.

Soon Liza's father was called by the police officer. After the phone call, he was upset. He sat in the living room

looking out the window. All he said to
Liza was, "Myers is coming over in two
hours." Then he didn't say anything else.

When Officer Myers came that
evening, he talked with Mr. Sutton in
the living room. Liza was in the den,
and she could hear them.

Officer Myers told Liza's dad all the bad things Ben, Jack, and Liza did. He said that the damage was serious this time. The police officer then said that Liza had been running wild for quite a while. She seemed to be neglected. Two other neighbors had told him about bad things Liza had done. He also reported, "The man at Miller Grocery said he thought Liza was stealing from the store, but he didn't catch her." Liza's father didn't say anything.

"Well," said Officer Myers to Liza's father, "what do you plan to do about this problem?"

"Liza will have to stay in for a week or two," Mr. Sutton said. "Maybe that will take care of it."

Officer Myers said, "No, I don't think keeping her at home will fix this problem."

Liza's dad said angrily, "Well, just what do you think *will* fix this problem?"

"Understanding why she is getting into so much trouble is a first step toward fixing it. We have a good mental health center," Officer Myers said.

"Wait just a minute here," Mr. Sutton said in a loud voice. "You have no right to stick your nose in our lives. We're just fine. I don't believe in that kind of help."

Then Officer Myers said to Liza's dad, "Look, you have two choices. You can get help for yourself and Liza and figure out why Liza is always in trouble.

Otherwise, I will present the things that Liza is doing in court. A judge will decide if she's being neglected, and if she is, what will happen. Let me know what you are going to do."

Officer Myers left after that. Liza's dad was really angry. He didn't like anyone telling him what to do. He slammed the door behind Officer Myers. Then he started to yell.

"Just who does he think he is?" he shouted. "A psychologist? What do psychologists know? Nothing! They just mess in people's lives."

Liza was scared. She hated it when he got so mad. So she quietly went off to her room and stayed there all night— without any supper.

The next morning her dad didn't go to work. He was still angry. She could tell. He didn't say a word all morning.

Finally, he growled, "Today we're going to visit this psychologist. We're going to find out why you are getting into trouble. Get ready! We're leaving at 9:30."

The psychologist they visited at the mental health center said her name was Eva. She told them that her job was to help people where she could and give help to people who wanted it. Then she asked Liza and her father to talk about themselves. Mr. Sutton was angry at first, and wouldn't talk much. But in a short while he seemed to like talking with Eva. Liza thought she liked Eva, too, but she decided to wait to see if Eva really was nice.

Mr. Sutton and Liza visited Eva for the next few months. Liza found that she could talk to Eva about many things. Eva asked Liza about the bad things she was doing. Liza wasn't sure why she did those things at first. But by talking, Liza found out that she was angry. No one took care of her during the day. She fixed most of her meals herself, since no one was there, and often just ate cereal or ice cream. No one wanted to come over to play with her because her house was dirty and messy all the time. Her clothes were always dirty, too, because Mr. Sutton didn't do the washing very often.

Most of all, Liza was angry that her mother died—angry and sad. Being sad hurt Liza a lot, so she only let herself be angry. When she hurt others, like her neighbors, she was showing how much she hurt on the inside.

Liza was also angry and sad about her father. He got quiet a lot and didn't talk to Liza. He neglected her—he didn't give her the things she needed, especially a chance to talk about her mother. With Eva's help, Liza and her father did talk about Liza's mother dying. Liza found out that her father was very sad, too. They both talked about missing her mother.

Liza's father was changing. He talked with Liza more than he did before.

Because he worked, he found a housekeeper to do many of the things that were not being done for Liza. This woman, Mrs. Wilson, made lunch and supper, cleaned the house, did the wash, and scolded Liza when she was late. Mrs. Wilson took good care of Liza. Now, Liza wasn't alone anymore during the day, and her dad was talking to her and taking better care of her.

Little by little, Liza stopped being so hurt and angry inside. She felt sorry about all the trouble she had made. The next summer, she helped some of her neighbors plant new gardens. The neighbors saw that Liza was changing.

"We sure like it now when you come over!" they said to Liza. She was glad about that.

# Children and Neglect

Liza's story is a true one. Liza was neglected. Her father didn't take good enough care of Liza. Here are some things to know about neglect.

- Neglect means that a child is not being cared for properly. Neglect is not being given things that should be given to every child. Neglect is against the law. It is also bad for children.

- You have a right to be taken care of. In the story, Liza was too young to stay home alone all day while her father worked. Until Mrs. Wilson came to help, no one was there to take care of Liza. Before Mrs. Wilson, Liza's father often didn't know where Liza went and what she was doing. That is a kind of neglect.

- You have a right to food and warm clothing. Liza's father didn't make her meals or wash her clothes very often. Some parents don't buy food or clothes for their children, even if they have the money. That is a kind of neglect.

- You have a right to see a doctor and a dentist when you need one. You also need to see them to be sure you stay healthy. When parents don't do this, especially when a child is sick or has a bad tooth, it is a kind of neglect.

- You have a right to an education. Some parents don't want their children to go to school. It's okay to keep children at home when a teacher teaches the children there, or when a child is sick and needs to stay home. But when parents keep their children home a lot without teaching them, or let the children skip school whenever they want to, it is neglect.

- You have a right to a home, a safe place to live. In the story, Liza's father didn't keep their house clean or fixed up so that it was a good place to live. If parents make their children live in a very dirty, unsafe, or dangerous place, it is neglect.

- Neglected children can come from almost anywhere—from rich and poor neighborhoods, from cities, towns, and farms, and from families of every color.

- The police are not always the ones who find out about children who are neglected. Usually, the Child Protection office does. The jobs of the police are to keep people safe and to keep people's things safe. In the story, Liza and her friends damaged other people's things—that's why they had to see Officer Myers.

- Not all parents see a psychologist when they neglect their children. Eva helped Liza's father learn about neglect in the story. Other parents can learn how to take better care of their children, and not neglect them, from social workers and other helpers.

- Almost all parents want to be good parents to their children. But a few just have too many problems and cannot learn to help their children grow to be healthy, happy, and safe. When parents cannot take good care of their children, the children are sometimes taken from their homes. They may go to live with a foster family or other family who will help the children grow up well. This only happens when family troubles are very bad.

- Not all children who are neglected get into trouble like Liza did. Some neglected children misbehave and do bad things. Others may be very quiet and never talk about their homes. When these children act in ways that are different from most children, it is often a way of asking for help. Neglected children could also ask someone to help them.

## Places to Get Help

If you think you are being neglected, or if you know someone who is neglected, you can ask for help. Here are some people or groups you could tell.

**The family:** Your parents
Aunts, uncles, or cousins
Grown-up brothers and sisters
Grandmothers and grandfathers
Guardians

**At school:** Teachers
Social workers
School nurses
Counselors
Friends

**In the city
or town:** Neighbors
Police officers
Someone from Child
Protection Services
Doctors or nurses

## Words to Know

**ashamed (uh·SHAYMD)**—when a person feels sorry about something he or she has done, or feels bad because people don't like what he or she has done

**behavior (bee·HAYV·yor)**—the way a person acts

**court (KORT)**—a meeting with a judge (and sometimes a jury) where the judge decides if someone has broken the law or if someone with serious problems should get help for those problems

**damage (DAM·uhj)**—here, *damage*

means when a thing is hurt or destroyed

**discipline (DIHS·ih·plihn)**—here,
*discipline* means telling a child how to
act by talking or by punishing the child

**judge (JUHJ)**—the person in charge of
the court who sees that the rules of the
court are obeyed, and who decides if
someone has broken the law or if
someone needs help for very serious
problems

**mental health center (MEN·tuhl HELTH
SEN·tuhr)**—a place where psychologists
and other people work with people who
have serious personal problems and try
to help those people solve their problems

**misbehave (mihs·bee·HAYV)**—to act in a way that most people would say is bad

**neglect (nuh·GLEKT)**—here, *neglect* means when a child's parents or guardians do not take good care of that child, and fail to give him or her enough food, clothes, housing, or schooling, or don't take the child to the doctor or the dentist

**police (poh·LEESS)**—men and women who work for the government whose jobs are to help people stay safe and to keep people's homes and things safe

**police station (poh·LEESS STAY·shuhn)**—the place where police officers work

**psychologist (sy·KAHL·uh·jist)**—a person whose job is to work with people to help them understand why they think, feel and act as they do, and who can help those people solve serious personal problems

**serious (SIHR·ee·uhs)**—here, when something is important in a bad way

**uniform (YOU·nih·form)**—clothes that are all alike

**unsupervised (uhn·SOO·per·vyzd)**—not watched over or taken care of

## Note to Adults

Neglect is difficult to define because of the different values people have regarding parenting. Therefore, it is often difficult to help neglected children. The definition of neglect varies from state to state, but generally it is defined as failure of a child's parent(s) or guardian(s) to supply the child with adequate food, shelter, clothing, education, or health care, even when financially able to do so.

In a survey of about 150 school children in Minneapolis, undertaken to evaluate knowledge of child abuse and neglect, we found that the children had a misconception that neglect is only a function of poverty—a misconception shared by many adults. While there is certainly neglect at every level of society, this book shows that middle-class parents can often be neglectful. Upper- and middle-class neglect usually takes the form of lack of supervision and parent involvement.

## How Adults Can Help

Parents who neglect their children need help in understanding that neglect is harmful, both physically and psychologically, to their children. Unfortunately, people are hesitant to recognize and intervene in neglect cases because of the need to maintain respect and privacy for families.

Therefore, only the severest cases of neglect tend to be dealt with. Most neglect goes unaided.

If a child you know is not receiving adequate care as defined by law, a report to local Child Protection authorities might be necessary. (The police usually become involved in such situations only when the neglect is life-threatening or when criminal behavior is involved.) Child Protection must investigate the reports they receive. If they find neglect, they will urge the parents or guardians to work on changing the situation, often with the help of mental health professionals.

However, if such urgings have no effect, there may be no other choice than to take the case to juvenile court. There, a judge may remove the children from the home and place them in foster care if the neglect of the children is chronic and severe enough.

Children have a right to be raised in a healthy, safe home. It's an adult responsibility to provide such an environment.

## About the Authors

Deborah Anderson, Executive Vice President of Responses, Inc., has helped establish programs to aid both children and adults whose lives have been touched by abuse and neglect. Deborah developed and directed a sexual assault services program for the Hennepin County (Minnesota) Attorney's Office, and created the conceptual basis for Illusion Theater's internationally acclaimed production, "Touch," which presents information on abuse to children. Deborah has worked with students, teachers, and school administrators regarding child abuse and neglect, and has been nationally recognized for her work in the area of children as victims or witnesses in court.

Martha Finne, Director of the Children's Division of Responses, Inc., joined that organization after directing a survey of Minneapolis school children entitled, "Child Abuse and Neglect: From the Perspectives of the Child," the basis for these books. She has worked as a child abuse consultant, speaking to parent groups and elementary school staffs regarding child abuse and its prevention. Her background includes a degree in social psychology, counseling at the Bridge for Runaway Youth, and volunteer experience working with both public schools and social service agencies.

## About Responses, Inc.

Responses to End Abuse of Children, Inc. is a public nonprofit corporation which tries to coordinate programs in all segments of the community aimed at reducing family violence and child abuse and neglect. The organization works with both the private and public sectors to develop the most constructive responses to these problems.

In 1983 and 1984 Responses, Inc. conducted a survey of Minneapolis school children to assess the children's knowledge on various aspects of child abuse and neglect. The responses to the survey provided the framework for these Child Abuse books.